by Ken Kinstle- Owner Kinstle and Sons Services LLC

This e-book is an excellent resource meant to educate and get you started in the Mortgage Field Inspection Service business.
It is not all inclusive or the final answer but a collaboration of my experiences in this business.

Kenneth Kinstle is the owner and operator of Kinstle and Sons Services
A thriving contracting, mortgage inspection and property preservation
company operating in the Black Hills of South Dakota USA
You can learn more about me by visiting my web site at
http://kenkinstle.com

You can also contact me at 605-391-3938 or
mrken77@gmail.com

Table of Contents

Introduction	**Page 3**
Requirements	**Page 7**
Inspection Types	**Page 8**
Procedures	**Page 16**
Company Lists	**Page 21**
Groups for Information	**Page 24**
Field Service Links	**Page 25**

Thank you for reading this. I hope it is as beneficial to you as it has been to my family and me over the past twenty years. Please visit my website that has some information and leave me a comment there!

Introduction

The Mortgage Field Service Inspections business is a
recession proof business opportunity!
The benefits of having a business as a Mortgage Field Service Inspector are the flexibility to create your own schedule and the opportunity to earn an extra income or a good full time income. This industry will give you the ability to be in control of your life again. Schedule your own work times and be your own boss.

Financial and insurance institutions nationwide have vested interests in homes, commercial property, and businesses they have loaned money against. They require regular information on these assets. Our business offers a list of services and you can also.

This field is in high demand because these institutions need to continuously have updated and accurate information on the condition of these properties. The current economic situation has developed has provided more opportunities for Field

Service Inspectors because homes and commercial properties that are being refinanced, foreclosed or are vacant, still require frequently updated photos and reports. Nationwide, lending, leasing and insurance institutions need to continuously have updated and accurate information on the condition on these properties.

These institutions need to contract out this work to National Field Service companies which hire freelance Field Service Inspection representatives all over the country. That is where you and I have an opportunity to build a business!

I have been in this business for over 12 years and it continues to provide a good income, plus I get to see all kinds of different locations. If you like being on the move this may be for you!

Being an independent contractor has both advantages and drawbacks. I believe that the advantages and opportunity far outweigh the draw backs.

The drawbacks of making a successful business are: hard work, self
motivation, and discipline. There are times when you don't receive a steady paycheck but still must make things work. There have been many times when I thought that it was time to get a job again. I am thankful I have not though.

I have been a business entrepreneur for over 20 years.

The advantages are: more time freedom and the ability to make more income. Building a business is the way to accomplish these things. The part of a business where people say you don't have a boss isn't really that accurate as I have customers and clients that are demanding. Still, I set my own hours and call my own shots that won't come with many jobs.

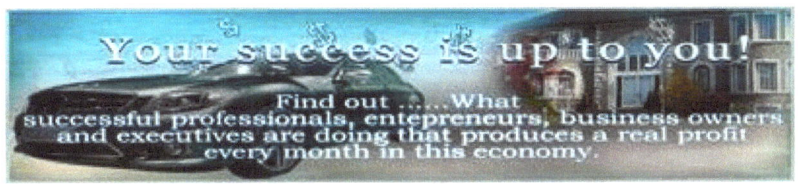

kenkinstle.com

You can start making $30- $5000.00 a month just inspecting properties for mortgage companies. Now is a great chance in the current market to get work in the mortgage inspection field!

When I originally wrote this in the first quarter of 2010 the economy was still very poor in a lot of locations, so the property preservation and mortgage inspection businesses are really producing. These are the types of businesses that are reverse linked to the economy.

If you have what it takes, these are great to get involved in. They are more than able to produce good income in our country today.

The Requirements

What does it take?

Mortgage inspections are probably the best way to start in the industry.

The requirements:
- PC- A Laptop or Desktop- It will need to be fairly up to date to use the client software. Most systems use windows based systems.
- Reliable Internet Connection
- Reliable Transportation
- Digital Camera
- Attention to detail
- Ability to read and follow simple directions
- Good Work Ethic and Self Discipline
- Insurance - Liability and Errors and Omissions Insurance-

(Requirements are different depending on client)

As you can see, the requirements are not burdensome to start this business. If you can meet these requirements and would like to consider this further, the next section will give you a list of services that you can provide.

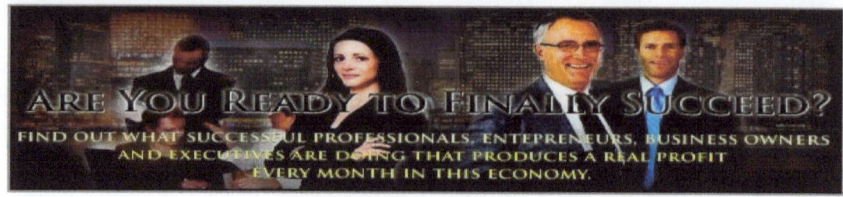

Inspection Types

This example list shows the services Kinstle and Sons provides
and gives you a brief overview on what you would be doing.
Kinstle and Sons Inspection Services include:

1. No Contact Inspection - This is the simplest of our services. It includes finding the correct property, taking a photo of the properties street elevation and a photo of the physical address. We visually verify occupancy without contacting mortgagor.

2. Property Inspection Report - This includes finding the correct property, taking a photo of the properties street elevation and a photo of the physical address. We then either contact the mortgagor, neighbor, or postal carrier to determine the properties occupancy.

3. Occupancy Verification - This includes finding the correct property, taking a photo of the properties street elevation and a photo of the physical address. We then either contact the mortgagor, neighbor, or

postal carrier to determine the properties occupancy.

4. REO Occupancy Status Inspection - This includes finding the correct property, taking a photo of the properties street elevation and a photo of the physical address. We then either contact the mortgagor, neighbor, or postal carrier to determine the properties occupancy.

5. Rush Inspection - This includes finding the correct property, taking a photo of the properties street elevation and a photo of the physical address. We then either contact the mortgagor, neighbor, or postal carrier to determine the properties occupancy. These have a rush due date and require faster processing. Most companies add a rush fee.

5. Evening Occupancy Verification - This includes finding the correct property, taking a photo of the properties street elevation and a photo of the physical address. We then either contact the mortgagor, neighbor, or postal carrier to determine the properties occupancy. This is performed in the evening hours attempting to contact mortgagor.

6. Sale Date Inspection - This includes finding the correct property, taking a photo of the properties street elevation and a photo of the physical address. We then either contact the mortgagor, neighbor, or postal carrier to determine the properties occupant. This type has to be completed on a set date: the date property is transferred.

7. Insurance Loss Inspection - This is to determine the extent of damages claimed by insured and/or the percentage of work that has been completed. This is one of the most intense inspections we perform. Companies want detailed photos, reports, and diagrams.

This is a brief overview of our inspection services that you could also offer!

==Here are more types that you could offer:==

Bankruptcy Inspection - A bankruptcy inspection is an objective visual analysis for determining the occupancy of a property where no contact is made with the mortgagor or property occupant. The inspection form typically requires you to provide a description of the property, how occupancy was determined, and exterior photographs of the property. This type of field inspection takes a couple of minutes to complete.

Broker's Price Opinion - A BPO provides the value of a property based on three comparable properties. Details about the condition of the property, neighborhood condition, and significant property distinctions that may affect the marketability of the property are provided by you, along with exterior (and interior) photographs of the property. A BPO can only be completed by a licensed real estate broker, and takes about 30 minutes to complete.

Compliance Inspection - A compliance inspection

determines if the repairs required by state and local regulations have been made to a property in order for escrow funds to be released. Each inspection form will usually require you to provide a description of the property, the percentage of repairs completed, and photographs of the repairs. This takes about 20 minutes to complete.

Condition Verification - A condition inspection is an objective visual analysis of a property to determine whether the property has sustained damage due to neglect or vandalism, or if liability hazards are present. A description of the property, any visible conditions or hazards, and photographs of the property are usually required. This takes a few minutes to complete.

Damaged Freight Inspection - An inspection of freight damaged that a claim has been filed on. You will be filling out the forms provided by the company, taking plenty of photos of the item(s) and shipment container, and the damage. This type of inspection usually pays well and needs to be completed within 72 hours of assignment.

Delinquency Interview - When the mortgagor of a property is behind in payments, the mortgage company may want to make direct contact with the mortgagor to find out the reason for the default. As the field inspector, you will be asked to contact the mortgagor to ask them a series of questions provided by the mortgage company. Sometimes the mortgage company will ask you to put the mortgagor on your mobile phone if the mortgagor is present, or leave a letter for them. Typically, there is an inspection form for you to complete along with photograph requirements. The time to complete this inspection varies.

Draw Inspection - A draw inspection is performed at various stages in a new construction project in order to assist the lender in releasing funds to the building contractor. Each inspection will require you to provide estimated percentages of completion along with related photographs of the work completed. This takes about 15 minutes to complete.

Environmental Inspection - An environmental inspection is a visual exterior inspection of a property to assess the overall property condition for environmental liabilities and hazards. Inspection forms usually require you to provide a description of the property, the presence of any environmental problems found, and photographs of the property. This takes about 10 minutes to complete.

Fannie Mae Inspection - For properties financed with Fannie Mae loans, certain requirements must be satisfied in order to comply with the inspection regulations of Fannie Mae. Each inspection usually requires a description of the property and photographs. This takes a few minutes to complete.

FEMA Inspection - When there is a Presidential Disaster Declaration, an inspection is performed to determine whether the property has sustained visible damage due to the disaster. Each inspection usually requires a description of the damages and related photographs. This takes a few minutes to complete.

Floor Plan Inventory - This inspection is used to verify the inventory of a product at a retail location by counting the number of products at the retail store. Generally there are no photograph requirements. The time to complete this type of inspection varies by the project.

Foreclosure Inspection - A foreclosure inspection is performed on a foreclosed property, and is essentially the same as a Bankruptcy Inspection.

Insurance Inspection - There are basically two types of insurance inspections: Interior/Exterior and Exterior Only. Insurance inspection includes details about the construction materials used in the exterior construction of the dwelling, along with the condition of the dwelling, and hazard assessments. Photographs of the address number, front and back of dwelling, interior (when requested), outbuildings, and any hazards or conditions observed on the property are normally required, along with taking measurements of the footprint of the dwelling to produce a diagram of the dwelling. It takes about 10 minutes to complete an Exterior Only inspection and about 30 minutes to complete an Interior/Exterior inspection.

Leased Equipment Verification - When a company leases equipment to a merchant, the leasing company usually wants to verify the location and condition of its leased equipment. The inspection will require the inspector to visit the property to photograph the equipment and property. Also, the inspector will take note the condition of the equipment, the equipment's serial numbers, and the property itself. The time to complete this type of inspection varies by project.

Loss Draft Inspection - When a homeowner sustains a loss on real property and files an insurance claim for that loss, a loss draft inspection is performed before funds are released to repair the damages. A loss draft inspection is essentially the same as a Draw Inspection.

Merchant Site Verification - When a merchant wants to accept credit cards and e-checks from its customers, the credit card processor wants to make sure that the merchant's business is legitimate. Additionally, a merchant site inspection is required by the Patriot Act. This inspection usually requires photographs of the business and completing an inspection form. This takes about 15 minutes.

Occupancy Verification - An occupancy inspection determines who is currently occupying a property from an objective visual determination. The names of the occupant, property manager, and real estate agent information are collected whenever possible. Each inspection usually requires a property description, how occupancy was determined, the name of the occupants if possible, and photographs of the property. This takes a few minutes to complete.

   Sale Inspection - A sale inspection is an objective visual determination of who is occupying a property on the sale date of a foreclosure. The names of the occupant, property manager, and real estate agent information are collected whenever possible. Each inspection usually requires a property description, how occupancy was determined, the name of the occupants if possible, and photographs. This takes about 10 minutes to complete.

   Sale Date Inspection - This type of inspection is the same as a
Condition Inspection, except that is performed only on the day a property is sold.

   Vacant Property Inspection - When a property is vacant and lock box-secured, property inspections can ensure compliance with federal regulations, local ordinances, and investor agreements. The inspection usually requires the completion of an inspection form, photographs of the property, details about any visible conditions, and hazards found. This takes about 20 minutes to complete.

Procedures - Getting Started
What you need to do to get started

You must submit a vendor application to the companies you are interested in working for. There is a list below of some good companies that I recommend. If available, the link to each company's vendor application is included.

Compile a list of companies you want to start with. Have their information in front of you. Most information can be found on the web or with a quick phone call.
Download or get the companies vendor application. Read and study all the information you can find that each company provides.
Fill out the application, be professional! Do a rough draft and then a final if you need to. Remember, these first contacts will be all that this company knows about you. Make it good!

Once you have submitted an application, call and start a relationship with the vendor services department of the company. It's to your benefit to find the vendor relations person and make contact ahead of time. Introduce yourself; tell them you are interested in working for their company and that an application is on the way. After making this contact by phone, follow up with an email thanking them. BE PROFESSIONAL, FRIENDLY AND BRIEF. These people are usually very busy and appreciate a friendly voice, but their time is valuable! If they need a representative in your area you will know as they will pick up the pace. If not, build on the relationship and call back once a month. Remember; BE PROFESSIONAL, FRIENDLY, AND BRIEF.

   Each company will have a list of requirements and some will give you a time frame to have certain insurance requirements. Every company is different so just focus on a few choice companies, fill out a vendor application, make contact, and repeat. Write down the person's name, phone number, and e-mail address to make a follow up call to the same person.
   You might need to have an EIN (Federal Employer Identification Number) to submit an application with some companies. You may request an EIN on the IRS Website: http://www.irs.gov/. The process is free and takes only a few minutes to issue one to you.
   Do as much research as you can before you contact them; know as much as you can!
   Remember, they may not need your help but if you are consistent in checking with them, and your application looks good, then when they get in a pinch you are on the list to call!

Procedures - Doing an Inspection
Here is where the fun starts!

Congratulations, you have your first inspection work! Wow. It is usually fairly simple. Usually :-)

You will be provided a form with the inspection type and information needed. READ IT thoroughly! That is the most important item since they will be different but have specific inspection types and instructions. If you see a type of inspection or instructions that you do not understand, just call and ask that vendor rep you built a relationship with (you did, right?). They are usually happy to help a new conscientious inspector get started!

First, identify the type of inspection, some may be contact, some will be NO CONTACT, it is important to know that. Legally in a bankruptcy the mortgagee can NOT make contact with the mortgagor. READ THE FORM!

Once you are sure of this, you will have a name address, loan number, and sequence (or inspection) number. Then you will do a search for the property on http://www.mapquest.com/ or http://maps.google.com/maps?tab=ml or any other good mapping program.

You will be able to find 98% of your inspections in this manner. What about the other 2%? Those can be fun! Ok, it will benefit you to develop a relationship with the assessor's office. This will be the best way to find a property that is not on the usual maps. You will find that MapQuest and Google seem to be almost two years behind and don't list newer developments. Do a Google search for the counties name and the assessor's phone number. Some counties will also have a GIS map that you can use. Start with the assessor's office and make friends with the person answering the phone since you may be calling them often.

Here are other resources to find a difficult address: post office, fire department, police department and even realtors. I have had to use all of these and the best is a friendly assessor's office because they have the information that you need. You will need to know the county (to get the correct assessor's office). The occupants name or the address is usually enough for them to give you directions right to the door. TIP- Write it down in detail and save it! Most likely you will need it again.

That can be the most difficult frustrating part of the work after you have some clients is locating a hard to find address. After that you will need to schedule and map out your route with the addresses that you must inspect. Some forethought and planning will save you much time and backtracking in the field. You may choose to use GPS to navigate your route and that is a topic for another day.

Double check your address upon arrival. Take a front picture of the property and a close up of the address on the property. This is a good time to check the inspection, and fill out all needed information.

Know ahead of time if it is a No Contact Inspection since you will want to determine occupancy and get a picture without making contact.

Remember this on your first inspection and on inspection #500,000: quality, quality, and remember quality. These first inspections as well as every inspection that you do subsequently will establish your reputation and your business. The level of quality you provide will determine your longevity and reputation with the companies you work for.

If you are honest, work hard, and pay attention to detail you can be very successful in this business.

Companies We Recommend:

Servicelink Black Knight

LPS is a national leader in field services is a LPS division recognized as a leading provider of integrated technology and services to the mortgage industry.
Inspections and Preservation Work

ServiceLink
1400 Cherrington Parkway
Moon Township, PA 15108
Toll Free: 800.777.8759
https://www.svclnk.com/vendor-info/

Integrated Mortgage Solutions

In the dynamic world of real estate, Asset Disposition and Management Services™ (ADAM) is an essential element of mortgage lending. Integrated Mortgage Solutions (IMS) provides a full range of asset management services from inspections, repair and preservation, hazard claims recovery, to loss mitigation, including borrower outreach, short sale management and REO services. It delivers them in a seamless way that smoothly integrates into our clients' operations.

16225 Park Ten Place, Suite 105
Houston, TX 77084
Phone: (281) 994-4500
Fax: (281) 994-4501
E-mail: contact@imstoday.com

http://www.imstoday.com/

Compass Claims Services, Inc.

Insurance Loss Inspections
7598 E. Palo Verde St Ste A
Prescott Valley, AZ 86314
Phone: (928) 759-3990
Email: info@compassclaims.com

http://www.compassclaims.com/

Asset Management Contacts

Valuation Support Services   https://www.vss20.com

Advantage Valuation   http://www.advantagevaluation.com/

Americas Infomart Inc.   https://www.aimyourway.com/

ASD America   http://www.asdamerica.com/inspections.htm

ASG Mortgage Services Inc.   http://www.asgbpo.com/

Mortgage Field Rep   http://www.mortgagefieldrep.com/

Asset Disposition Management, Inc.   http://www.admreo.com/

Phoenix Asset Management, LLC
http://www.assetonemg.com/Website/index.html

Asset Valuation & Marketing Inc.   http://www.assetval.com

Atlas REO Services   http://www.atlasreo.com

Bank of Rio Vista   http://www.bankofriovista.net/

Bank of the Orient   http://www.bankorient.com/home/

Bank of the Pacific http://www.bankofthepacific.com/

Important Field Service Links and Information

Field Inspector Training
http://www.fieldinspectortraining.com/

Property Preservation Forum
http://www.propertypreservationforum.com

NewRep
Free advertising for Field Service companies
http://www.newrep.com

Netronline
Find assessors office numbers or websites
http://publicrecords.netronline.com/

InspectorADE
Inspection Software
http://www.inspectorade.com

Related Forums and Groups

Mortgage Field Services is a group for property preservation and inspection professionals. If you are interested in networking, learning about, or contributing to Mortgage Field Services topics... this is the place.
http://finance.groups.yahoo.com/group/mortgagefieldservices/

http://finance.groups.yahoo.com/group/Insurance-and-Mortgage-Field-Services/

http://finance.groups.yahoo.com/group/Field-Service-Reps-Wanted/

Inspection and Preservation Companies and Links

Advanced Field Services Reporting
25531 Commerce Drive #110, Lake Forest, CA 92630, 949-597-9021, Fax 619-563-2450,
http://www.afsweb.com

Advanced Mortgage Solutions
US-wide - providing property preservation, inspections, insurance claims/repairs, appraisals, title work and sales.
http://www.advancedmortgagesolutions.com/

America's InfoMart, Inc.
US-wide - providing inspections, BPO's, appraisals, evictions, mobile notary signings, and property preservation. Complete services listed.
http://www.quickbpo.com/

Ann Michaels and Associates
US-wide - mystery shopping, integrity shops, sales training for small, mid-sized and large customers.
http://ishopforyou.com/Home_Page.html

AppIntell Inc.
US-wide - providing risk management information and data analysis solutions and tools to the lending industry.
http://www.appintelligence.com/

ASD America, Inc.
US-wide - offers complete property management, including inspections, preservation and protection, marketing and sales of REO properties.
http://www.asdamerica.com/

Big Apple Inspections
New York - offering residential, commercial, insurance and HUD REAC inspections in New York Metropolitan and Long Island areas.

http://www.bigappleinspections.com/

Buczek Inc.
Western New York - providing service to HUD, VA, banking institutions, Real Estate firms, apartment owners, and other servicing companies.
http://buczek-inc.com/

C & A Preservation, Inc.
California – providing preservation service since 1993 including re-keys, lawn cuts, boarding, pool draining, rehab, debris removal, and on site inspections of all kinds.
http://capreservation.biz/

Cavanaugh & Company, LLC
Connecticut - offers property inspections, preservation, REO management, and notary services.
http://www.cavanaughandcompany.com/

A City Suburban Service, Inc.
Illinois - Chicago area - property inspection, evictions and preservation services, including debris removal, board-ups, painting services. Roll-off container rental in Chicago and the six collar counties around it.
http://www.city-suburban.com

Classic Mortgage Services
Oklahoma - property preservation and inspection services since 1989.
http://www.classicmortgageservices.net/

Clear Capital
US-wide - providing real estate valuation and due diligence services; BPOs, AVMs, AVM hybrids, and property inspections.
http://www.clearcapital.com/

Collateral Specialists

US-wide - commercial site inspections.
http://www.collateralspecialists.com/

Collateral Verifications Inc.
US-wide - provider of aircraft appraisals and on site asset inspection services for all industries.
http://www.i-collateral.com/

Countrywide Field Services Corporation
US-wide - providing inspections, evictions, securing, and property preservation.
http://www.ctcres.com/

CPM Services
USA, Inc. - New York State - providing inspections, property preservation, lawn maintenance, board-ups, evictions, demolition, and extermination services.
http://www.cpmservices-usa.com/

Cyprexx Services
Southern US – provides debris removal. Also provides discount flooring and appliances for foreclosure properties.
http://www.cyprexx.com/

Denali Ventures, Inc.
US-wide - providing services for REO properties.
http://www.denaliventures.com/msihome.aspx?t=54

Ann Michaels and Associates - US-wide - mystery shopping, integrity shops, sales training for small, mid-sized and large customers.

Field Service Companies

- AppIntell Inc. - US-wide - providing risk management information and data analysis solutions and tools to the lending industry.
- ASD America, Inc. - US-wide - offers complete property management, including inspections, preservation and protection, marketing and sales of REO properties.
- Asset One Marketing Group - US-wide - asset management and disposition firm offering specialized services to financial institutions, financial services companies and mortgage servicers.
- Berger Enterprises, LLC - Wisconsin - full-spectrum inspection agency serving insurance companies and financial institutions.
- Big Apple Inspections - New York - offering residential, commercial, insurance and HUD REAC inspections in New York Metropolitan and Long Island areas.
- Buczek Inc. - Western New York - Serving HUD, VA, banking institutions, Real Estate firms, apartment owners and other servicing companies.
- C & A Preservation, Inc. - California - preservation service since 1993 including re-keys, lawn cuts, boarding, pool draining, rehab, debris removal and on site inspections of all kinds.
- Cavanaugh & Company, LLC - Connecticut - offers property inspections, preservation, REO management and notary services.
- A City Suburban Service, Inc. - Illinois - Chicago areas - property inspection, evictions and preservation services - including debris removal, board-ups, painting services. Roll-off container rental in Chicago and the 6 collar counties around it.
- Classic Mortgage Services - Oklahoma - property preservation and inspection services since 1989.
- Clear Capital - US-wide - providing real estate valuation and due diligence services; BPOs, AVMs, AVM hybrids, and property inspections.
- Collateral Specialists - US-wide - commercial site

inspections.
- Collateral Verifications Inc. - US-wide - provider of aircraft appraisals and on site asset inspection services for all industries.
- Cyprexx Services - Southern US - Debris removal. Also provides discount flooring and appliances for foreclosure properties.
- Direct Contact USA, Inc - Field services group. Includes information on notary and property preservation services.
- Douglas-Guardian Services - US-wide - provides lenders with collateral verification and inspection services.
- Eagle Inspection Services, Inc. - Mid-west tri-state coverage for lender servicing related needs.
- Eagle Inspections of Michigan - Michigan - providing property preservation and field inspections. Service area map.
- Fast Snap - Your Online Photographer - California - offers photos of homes, offices, stores, apartment buildings, factories, bridges, roads, and intersections.
- FCI - US-wide - offering lenders or servicers outsourcing for debt preservation, collection, and default processes.
- Fidelity National Field Services, Inc. - US-wide - property preservation, inspections, title services since 1968.
- Field Asset Services, Inc. - US-wide - a full service preservation company providing eviction assistance and REO maintenance.
- Field Services, Inc. - US-wide - manufactured housing field service inspections and winterization. Skip tracing services also provided.
- First American Field Services - US-wide - property inspection and preservation services for the mortgage industry.
- First Preston - US-wide - portfolio marketing, management and sales for institutional investors, mortgage banking firms, government agencies and other clients.

- Five Brothers Mortgage Company Services and Securing - US-wide - inspections, evictions and property preservation.

- Flamingo Net - Southeast Florida - provides inspection services and inspector training manual.
- Goodman Dean Corporate Real Estate Services - US-wide - complete asset management services.
- GS Property Management & Home Improvements, LLC - North and central New Jersey - offering inspections, maintenance, and home improvement services to residential, real estate, banking, mortgage, and foreclosure industries.
- Guardian Portfolio Services, Inc - St. Petersburg, FL - field verification and collection services.
- The Hauser Group - US-wide - mystery shopping, mail tracking, telemarketing phone monitoring, product comparison.
- His Will Property Services Inc. - Northeast US tri-state property preservation and management firm. Management solutions for residential and commercial properties.
- I.C.O.M. Enterprises - NE, MO, KS - Property inspections, preservation, securing, winterization, insurance loss drafts, debris removal.
- Imagine Service Group, Inc. - Florida - Statewide inspections and preservation services including lock changes, winterization, lawn care, eviction assistance and minor/major rehab.
- Ingeprom, Inc. - Puerto Rico - Integrating project management, property management and field maintenance services.
- InspectNet - US-wide - construction and real estate risk management services.
- Jerry R Devorss & Associates - Massachusetts - property inspection services including merchant site and insurance loss drafts.
- JR Services, LLC - Ohio - complete services for delinquent to foreclosed asset. Also offers training course and business consulting for new start-ups.
- Keystone Asset Management - US-wide - REO Management includes occupancy status, cash for keys programs, evictions, securing and re-keying, moving, property storage, BPO's and Appraisals.

- Kinnamon Group, Inc. - US-wide - REO servicer providing inspections, collections, property preservation, asset management, rehab and liquidation.
- Landmark Contractor Services, Inc. - Ohio statewide - full service property preservation company, lock changes, winterization, eviction services, and board-ups. US-wide - property preservation billing services for contractors.
- Landsafe, Inc. - US-wide - providing a variety of inspections for buyers, sellers, realtors and mortgage bankers.
- Lenders Asset Management Corp. - US-wide - foreclosure and asset management including evictions and property preservation of single and multi-family residences, land, and commercial properties.
- Lighthouse Real Estate Solutions - US-wide - REO disposition, property preservation and inspection services.
- M & M Mortgage Services - US-wide - field inspections and property preservation for the mortgage industry.

- Mackay Group, Inc. - New York state - provides default management services for lenders.
- Maryland Real Estate Services, Inc. - Maryland, Delaware and District of Columbia - providing property inspections and preservation, specializing in evictions.
- McDaniel Contracting Inc - Atlanta Georgia area - offering services to real estate agents and mortgage brokers who specialize in REO, distressed and foreclosed properties.
- McDargh Real Estate Services - US-wide - commercial property inspections, site reports, real estate due diligence, and mortgage field services.
- Michaelson, Connor & Boul - US-wide - services include but are not limited to BPO, REO marketing and disposition, appraisals, property management and inspections.
- Millennium Services - US-wide including Puerto Rico, Guam and the Virgin Islands - provides inspection and property preservation services.
- Mortgage Contracting Services - US-wide - property inspection and preservation services.
- Mortgage Information Services - US-wide - offers title

searches, appraisals and loan closing services.
- Mortgage Specialist Inc - US-wide - offering delinquency interviews, property inspections and property preservation services.
- National Creditors Connection - US-wide - field services for the lending industry.
- National Field Representatives, Inc. - US-wide - provides inspections, property preservation, evictions, cash for keys, and other field services .
- National Foreclosure Services - US-wide - foreclosure services including evictions, cash-for-keys, property preservation, and appraisals.
- National REO Services, Inc. - US-wide - REO services including inspections, securing, preservation, repair services, BPO's, and appraisals.
- National Vendor Management Services - US-wide - providing commercial and residential property inspection services to the mortgage and insurance industries.
- Nationwide Appraisal Services - US-wide - appraisal and title management company providing valuation, REO, title, settlement, title insurance and escrow services.
- NewRep.com - US-wide - free listing directory of companies providing property inspection and preservation services, broker price opinions, or general contractor services.
- Northern New England Field Services - Inspects real estate and vehicle inventory. Also offers property assessments and property preservation services.
- One West Realty Group, LLC - Missouri - St. Louis and Kansas City Metro areas - offers REO sales, asset management, residential and commercial services.
- Organization of Real Estate Professionals - Errors and Omissions insurance for home inspectors, appraisers, mortgage field services and other real estate professionals.
- Pacific Field Service, Inc. - US-wide - offering commercial and residential property inspections.
- PB Inspections - US-wide - FEMA and residential insurance inspections.
- PCI-West Property Preservation - Utah and Idaho - providing

preservation and inspection services.
- PLM Lender Services, Inc. - California and Nevada - full service outsourcing. BPO, re-key, and evictions.

- Premier Field Services, LLC - Northeast Ohio clean-outs, lawn services and inspections.
- Pro Clean Out - Property maintenance company that has served the broker, mortgage, banking and foreclosure community. Includes information on services and coverage area.
- Pro-teck - US-wide - providing real estate and insurance appraisal services.
- Quality Assurance Consultants - US-wide - mystery shopping and cost controls.
- Quick Silver Messenger Service - California - process serving, delinquency interviews, bankruptcy, foreclosure, insurance loss, merchant site inspections.
- Ralph Cabal Inspection Services - Miami, FL - providing residential and commercial field services.
- Real Estate Owned Management, Inc. - Provides delinquency interviews, property inspections, repairs, and other inspection-related services in the United States, US Virgin Islands, and Puerto Rico.
- Real Estate Services Group - Southern California - mortgage field services and commercial property inspection.
- Red A Ranch Field Maintenance Co. - Southern California - property preservation and maintenance, first time vacants, board ups, and evictions. All loan types including FHA, FHMC, VA, FNMA, CONV loans.
- Reliance Field Services - Inspections, preservation, insurance loss, vehicle inspections, eviction assistance. United States.
- REM Corporation - US-wide - BPO's, appraisals, market evaluations, portfolio evaluations, title searches, and REO sales.
- REO Allegiance Inc. - US-wide - eviction moving and storage, debris removal, property preservation, winterization.
- REO Express - Florida and New York - licensed real estate broker providing BPOs, inspections and property

preservations.
- Reo Illinois - Illinois - offering REO disposition, liquidation, foreclosure services, management and marketing, inspections, valuations, and property preservation services.
- REO Maintenance - Michigan state wide preservation services.
- REO Nationwide - US-wide - providing default management, loss mitigation and liquidation of REO properties.
- REO Network - US-wide - pay for listing directory of REO foreclosure brokers, vendors, attorneys, and service companies.
- REO Servicing - Pennsylvania - servicing the greater Pittsburgh area with property preservation and REO management.
- Safeguard Properties, Inc. - US-wide, providing inspections, preservation and construction repair for foreclosed and REO property.
- Sam's Maintenance Services - Ohio - offers property preservation and inspections; on-line ordering and zip-code listing provided.
- Service Link, LP - US-wide - provider of closing, title and appraisal services.
- 24 Seven Services - Midwest MI - services include inspections, property preservation, repairs, mold abatement, and carpet cleaning.
- Snow Company - US-wide - inspection services for lender, realtor, or insurer.

- Society of Field Inspectors - US-wide - offers industry newsletter, networking, directory services.
- Society of Independent Representatives (S.I.R.s) - US-wide - not for profit association for independent representatives that perform field services. Offers free listings in their on-line directory.
- Source One Services - US-wide - real estate valuation services, BPO's and appraisals.
- Sprint Mortgage Services - US-wide - default interviews, occupancy status, insurance loss draft, commercial

inspections, BPO and appraisals, property preservation, evictions.
- Superior Home Services - US-wide - hazard insurance recovery and repair of damaged properties in the foreclosure and conveyance process.
- Texas Home Solutions - Houston, Texas - offering property preservation and repair services in all trades and disciplines.
- Turn of the Century - US, Canada, and UK - providing a wide range of field services.
- U. S. Property & Appraisal Services Corp. - US-wide - offering appraisals, preservation services, flood zone certification, radon and termite inspections.
- Western Territory Inc. - Denver Colorado to Wyoming - offering property inspection services for mortgage and insurance purposes.
- W-M Group, Inc. - US-wide - REO services including BPO's, valuations, cash-for-keys, evictions and management, occupancy verification, property preservation and sales.
- WolfPac Property Services, Inc. - New Hampshire and parts of Maine - property preservation and management including evictions.
- Wolverine Real Estate Services - US-wide - provider of property inspection and preservation services, and rehab.
- Wood's Property Services - Pennsylvania, Delaware, and Maryland - offers care and maintenance of vacant homes.
- Yahoo Groups - Property Preservation - US-wide - networking and leads for those offering and hiring property preservation companies.
- York-Jersey Underwriters, Inc. - US-wide - providing liability and errors and omissions insurance for the mortgage field service industry.

If you need further help please email me at mrken77@gmail.com

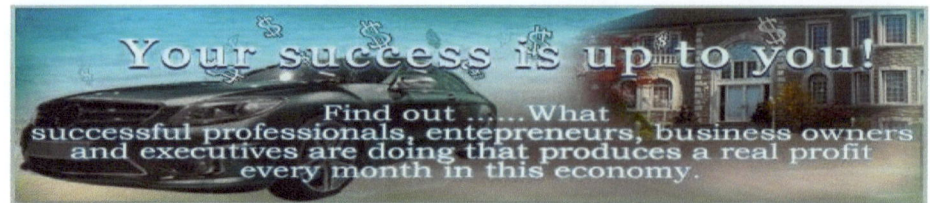

http://kenkinstle.com

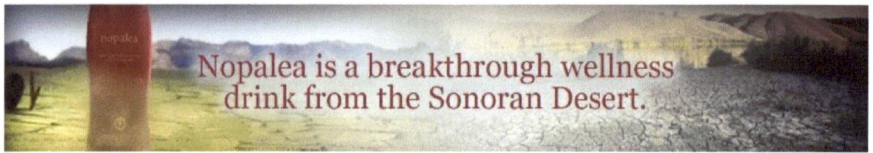

Health and Wellness Business
https://goo.gl/euc6hS

Bitcoin Profits
https://goo.gl/2fgXlK

www.ingramcontent.com/pod-product-compliance
Lightning Source LLC
Chambersburg PA
CBHW041117180526
45172CB00001B/287